Who am I When I'm Not Watching?

Nicholas Dolan

BookLeaf Publishing

India | USA | UK

Presentation by *BookLeaf Publishing*

Web: www.bookleafpub.com

E-mail: info@bookleafpub.com

ISBN: 9789360944209

First edition 2024

To Mom & Dad,

for cheering for me from the sidelines, from afar, or right by my side. And for passing down my artistic abilities. Thank you for truly everything. I love you both

ACKNOWLEDGEMENT

My always beautiful and encouraging Molly -Thank you for being my rock through this journey and for assisting me along the way. You make me a better me (and with that- a better writer). I love you dearly.

identity

Who am I
When I'm not watching?

lion's anxiety

2

I tell myself:

Even a lion's heart
Speeds up
Before the roar

i thought grey goose bottles could make me fly

We believe the answer to all
Life's problems
Are engraved in the bottom of
Glass bottles
And we may not understand
How ships fit in
But we're envious
How they find shelter
In the same place
We keep trying to make home

second chances

4

You know they have grocery stores
Filled with damaged goods
Salvaged, told they were unsellable
-Dented cans, warped boxes
Barely expired nutrients-
She sobbed her first time there
Saying
Everyone deserves a second chance like this

the lawn up the street

Sometimes
Hope isn't around the corner
But up the street

Sometimes
Resiliency is a push-mower
With an unsecured pull-cord
And life is a lawn

insides

6

Confidence
Doesn't always have to be
Frosting on cupcakes
It can be
The jelly inside a doughnut

pacifist

For the pacifist to pass a fist,
They train muscles to swallow their pride
Fight or flight becomes talk or walk
Are they impressed by strength
Only when it flexes
But not when it relaxes?

dissects

8

The right mindset
Sets you up for success

You're the lavender scent
That dissects my stress

tan

9

The way
Your dimples hold
Sunshine
I get tan
Looking at
Your smile

i still believe it

We walked by the ocean
And I took a photo of you
Not because the water sparkled in a way
That made diamonds dull but because
You made the ocean disappear
Suddenly waves were silent
I don't remember if the sun existed
You embodied it all
I audibly said
'This might be the best picture ever taken'
And I still believe it

the dirt & dust we collect

11

Love is knowing
All the nuclear codes
That could obliterate each other
But
Letting each of those buttons
Collect dirt and dust

the first date

Harvard Square bar.
I circled the neighborhood, looking for parking
When I walked in, I instantly spotted the waves
of your hair
Slightly past your shoulders, just like in your
pictures
You reached out to shake my hand
We both laughed at the awkwardness
Immediately, you tucked your hair behind your
right ear
I ran my hand through mine
Your voice was the perfect pitch
That could beautify Apple Media Services
Terms & Conditions
(Pantone certified eyes)
The way your dimples stayed
After you laughed at my rambling stories
You didn't just ask surface-level questions
(Work, family, school, hobbies)
You dove into the pool of my existence
With questions about my thoughts and emotions
When I reciprocated them back
You turned your chair slightly in my direction
So I could see your lips better
So I could see the crinkles cradle your eyes

You smelled like forever and I hardly knew you

When I went to the bathroom, I texted one of my
best friends
I almost called every news station in
Massachusetts
I couldn't contain my bliss, nor did I try
As I returned to you, you jumped back in
We had so much in common
I could never list them all here-
Your genuineness and sincerity transported me
to a utopia
In real-time, I felt my anxious heartbeat come to
a soft lull
Then pick back up to marching band level
(Hollywood's version of love at first sight may
not be far-fetched)

An instant fondness and affinity for you
I told you I loved your nickname, and did my
best Elton John rendition;
"'Gwynie' and the Jets"
I sang with unwavering confidence unfamiliar to
my skin
You touched my arm in a manner that suggested
My comedic choice paid off
Those dimples, that laugh
You were over-the-mantel frame-worthy

It was a school night for us, already after 10:30
When we hugged goodbye, I said let's do this
again soon
You agreed, with those dimples highlighted by
the streetlights

As I drove away, I immediately called my best
friend
Saying, I'm alive again for the first time in
months
I was revitalized by today

You became the ne plus ultra of first dates
How could we top Mount Everest?

...We couldn't. We didn't
Because I never saw you again.
Just that one time
That one night
The first date

by love

When you are motivated by love,
You'll solve the equation
That has scratched the back of your
consciousness
For as long as you have
Had feeling in your toes

You can't breathe without it

You love with the existence of color
Expression and wonder

Indisputable

More than any blade of grass
Drops on water's top
Love is capable

By love, we see hope
In everyone's potential

catastrophic

Catastrophe!
The moment you said, "We need to talk..."
My brain sent the wrong orders
To the wrong organs
The moment I saw your eyes look through me
I could feel myself being erased in real time
The moment I knew this was it...

Old televisions used to fade as they shut off
New ones go dark instantly
-So did we

counterfactual definiteness

When she asked about a second date, I expressed
I couldn't
Due to
"Counterfactual definiteness"
When she asked what that meant, I said:
          "What if we fell in love?
Spent months, years, studying each other's
Traits.   Talents.   Quirks.   Flaws.
Met each other's families and adored the little
ones
You would start to get an itch you can't scratch
From beyond the horizon to
'Objects in mirror are closer than they appear'
As your appetite slowly dwindled,
My taste buds would still crave you
You would develop a more sophisticated palate
Like suddenly 'the usual' at our favorite cafe
Would cause an allergic reaction
We'd make eye contact but see contrasting
visions
One of hope and forever
One of e s c a p i s m
                    ...eventually, you would
leave me...
So, I've been a part of such experiments before

The trials and tribulations
And with prognostication
I can't go through heartbreak again"

beacon

Where is their Beacon?
They search
The scouring hour of dusk

(What options exist for someone
Unknowing of their destination?)

A turn taken without knowing where it leads
Turning with onward intention,
The Beacon becomes
The Faith

Faith

Do they believe without seeing?

"Darkness is not a presence,
it is just the absence of light"

it's not the size of the fish in the ocean, it's the size of the ocean in the fish

For all they know,
The fish in the pond
Believe they're in the ocean

tim the stick

My therapist asked
When was the first time I noticed
That pattern…

I told her about a time in my youth
(I was probably 5 or 6)
At my grandparent's lake house in Maine
When I was playing in the water and
accidentally cut my foot
On a little stick
Being the precocious child I was, I found the
stick in the water
and introduced myself
and brought him inside the house to dry off
As my parents cleaned and bandaged my wound
They asked what I had in my hand
I told them it was the stick that hurt me
I named him Tim
My parents asked no more questions; they were
used to me

For the rest of the weekend, Tim was with me:
Coloring on the back porch
The dinner table seated between my brother and
I

The car ride into town
Even back playing in the water where we first
met
I forgave Tim for hurting me, then kept him
close
That is, until we left the lake house and I left
Tim in the yard
I knew I couldn't bring a stick home with me

So, when you ask when did I first notice this
pattern
Of keeping people around after they hurt me
...I think I've been this way for so long

i feel

I feel
   Like lightning in a bottle
   And like whiskey on ice

I feel
   Like hardcover novels
   And one grain of rice
   Like passion fruit gummy snacks
   In the shape of a star
   Like rides around the cul-de-sac
   The way lovers are

I feel
   Like fragments of a saint
   All I ever do is sin, spackle, repent

I feel
   Some peace and quiet
   Like midnight airport terminals
   Like thunder in your ribs
   Any sport convertible

I feel
   Like every color in the rainbow, silenced
   Letters in profanities, seeking asylum

Subtle golf claps when I speak of triumphs
Like green apple liqueur
A gut feeling ignored
I feel
Like a filament of myself
Never will admit to my health
That I feel like a beehive on fire
I defy my friar
I feel like my necklace is barbed wire

I feel I'm just another sinner
I feel like motifs and allegories
Like Aesop's Fables or Scattergories
Like metaphors or court orders

I feel
Like more to come-
I feel
I'm almost done-

one in a zillion

My love is ever-flowing
Broken nose bleed
My love is needle sewing
Sock when the toes freed

Your love is apple orchards
Your love is victories
I hang on all your words
We're making histories
Ones we will tell our children
And they will tell their children
This life that we are building
Is one in a zillion

our inventors

My parents invented everything

Before I met them, I knew nothing
Music didn't exist until my parents sang
Stories had never been told
I can't help but wonder
What we inherit
Must be the ability to not only
Create life
But to
Create everything